Foreword

JoRae – JOY Project Manager

CW01500433

I have been working for The JOY Pro, ..., ...
for over 3 years and I am continually humbled and honoured by the
women I meet on the project, their life stories, their vulnerability and
their resilience.

Any woman, and female identifying, can refer or be referred into the
project and for a whole range of reasons. We have women who come
for a cuppa and chat every week, maybe are lonely, or have been
bereaved, want to learn a new skill or craft and we have many varieties
of arts and crafts, or engage in physical classes from yoga to Zumba and
dance. We have women who want or need support to contact another
service, gain new employment and / or training programmes or
support for energy issues, benefits or housing or grants. In order to refer
women into the most appropriate services, we partner with many other
agencies. We support women who have low level mental health issues
like anxiety or low self-esteem for example to attend our project, as do
women who are neurodiverse (ADHC or ASC), women who have left
abusive relationships, or women who have moved area and don't know
anyone else. The list goes on and on. We have a volunteer programme
where women can start building back their confidence by meet and
greeting new women into the project, to women who run some of the
sessions themselves, come along and see where you go from there!
I am so excited because the project is moving into North and South
Worcestershire in 2023 and in 2024 we will also be launching a male
and identifying only space across the county too – it's a great time to
be a part of this awesome charity – why not get in touch and see where
your Journey will lead to? joy@worcestercommunitytrust.org.uk

This book was born from a conversation with amazing local writer
Holly Winter-Hughes and the JOY women who had been working on a

creative writing course together. The JOY Project motto is 'Your Journey'. So many of the extraordinary women who come to access JOY have such remarkable stories and poetry all waiting to be heard and here are so generously sharing their stories with you.

We hope you enjoy this collection of writing, artwork and self-care tips. JOY have delighted in creating it!

So, I invite you to make yourself a favourite drink, get comfy in a lovely place you like to sit or lie and enjoy the Journey you are about to embark on within the pages of this book.

This project was originated by The JOY Project and The Word Association with support from our friends at Crave Arts

CONTENT WARNING
This book deals with subjects that some readers may find distressing, such as sexual violence and abuse. Please read with care.

First published in the United Kingdom in 2023.
© The Word Association 2023
Each writer has asserted their right under the Copyright,
Designs and Patents Act, 1988 to be identified as the
author of their work.

All rights reserved.

This book or any portion thereof may not be reproduced
or used in any manner whatsoever without the express
written permission of the publisher except for the use of
brief quotations in a book review.
First published in the United Kingdom in 2023
by Bite Poetry Press.

www.the-word-association.com

ISBN 978-1-915787-94-1

First Edition

Cover image by Nash – www.nashfineart.com
Design by Gerard Winter-Hughes
www.winterhughes.com

Printed and bound in the UK by Biddles, Castle House East
Winch Road, King's Lynn PE32 1SF

UNHEARD VOICES
OUR JOURNEY TO JOY

Featuring the work of:

Amanda, Marina, Louise, Amelia, Jeanette, Michelle, Vicky, Debbie, T, Cassie, Michelle and Nash.

Generously funded by
The National Lottery's Community Fund

Produced by
The Word Association
with

CONTENTS

"I AM A **WOMAN** WHO HAS **REDISCOVERED** HER **VOICE...**"

We Are Fearless Women
Collaborative Poem

I was a trapped woman with no voice.
I was a scared woman, thinking I wouldn't get out alive.
I was a sick woman, who needed to run.

I was a trapped, fearful woman in need of help.
I was a despairing woman, thinking there was no way out.
I was an upset woman, life didn't allow me what I wanted.

I was a trapped, overwhelmed woman, feeling unheard.
I was a terrified woman, feeling dizzy with unease.
I was a lonely woman, thinking I was always going to live
in the dark.

I became a nervous woman, scared of the world.
I became a scared woman, not sure how to leave.
I became a broken, dumbstruck woman.

I became anxious, but ready to fly free.
I became a hopeful woman, ready to start again.
I became thankful.

I became energised.
I became a woman, in charge of her own future.
I became a successful artist, through my own efforts and
determination.

I became understood.
I became useful.
I became empowered.

I am a woman who is getting her life back on track.
I am a powerful woman.
I am a free woman.

I am a woman who is not scared anymore, the world is now my playground.
I am a woman who has rediscovered her voice.
I am a woman who believes in herself.

I am a woman, free from regret.
I am a fearless woman.
I am an inspired woman... I finally am a woman with her own identity.

Illustration by T

"I AM **GREEN,** I AM LOVE, I AM **GENTLY NURTURING LIFE**"

I Am a Woman With Power...

Having fought the conventional line

From a childhood in silence

To adulthood amongst trees and clouds

I know the expanse of my Power

No longer to shrink

My purpose more clear

To protect the source of my Power

Our world

Our home

Our Power

I Am Obsidian

I am green, I am love, I am gently nurturing life, absorbing the sun and the moon's energy, the light, drawing nutrients from the earth to pass on.

I am daisy, uncomplicated, natural, swaying in the breeze, strength in flexibility.

I am rabbit, my Chinese sign, very much my nature, avoiding the limelight, but quietly keeping busy. Observant and inquisitive.

I am obsidian. I am strong, repelling bad negative energy, protective.

I am Dunraven Bay, my go to place in my youth, evolving with time, certain and reliable. Tide coming in, tide going out... exhilarating and exciting. Clean and bright.

I am cliff. Not so permanent. Evolving, changing the landscape.

I am oak. Mature and beautiful. Reliable in its protection and shade, long living.

I am autumn. Soft and mellow, gentle, beautiful colours.

I am blackbird, a singer, an early riser, delighting those who are listening.

I am dawn, gently starting the day and setting things up for the time ahead.

Letting Go

I Was...

Frustrated, invisible, grieving for a life lost. A person no longer expressed. No longer able to use the skills and knowledge of a lifetime, having lost my place and position within my life.

I Am...

Taking small steps.

Joy brought me perspective; Joy helped me to find my voice and coaxed that voice back to life.

Joy brought me the courage to reassert my position and power.

Joy renewed my faith in my own power, the power to enquire, question and challenge once again.

I am able to choose, to put myself first, to let go of things that do me harm, to let go of that which no longer brings me joy, to speak my mind without fear. To feel joy without guilt.

What I want people to know about me...

I am not an open book

Most think I am

Though I cannot lie

And the emotion in my face will always give me away.

I do not judge and I will not

Respect those who do.

Respect must be earnt.

Actions not words, are my

Currency.

I forgive freely but never

Forget.

I am obsessed with the moon,

And hares, rabbits, trees and nature.

I love to pass on knowledge

To help heal and understand,

To unite, to empower,

And to celebrate life and love

With music and food.

Liberty Frog

Liberty frog. From my best friend.

A gift, so soon after we met.

Still cherished after three decades.

Our lives spent mostly apart

Always connected.

Our traumas shared,

Such parallel lives.

Liberty frog, a focus

For our shared thoughts,

Troubles and cares.

Laughter, love, tears and joy.

Don't Judge!

Don't judge, my Darling!
Dad's mantra.
Brought me pleasure, joy and pain.

Don't judge!
Forgot my instinct,
INTUITION DULLED.

Don't judge!
Makes life interesting, varied,
Caring, connected, joy.
Don't judge!

We are one species.
Don't judge!

My Pink & White Pal

When the day's been bleak

Or my mood black

I turn to my pink and white pal.

He's soft and silent.

His kindness, unspoken

but still expressed.

He mops up my tears.

No sigh, nor attempt to console.

Not spoken over, he warms

My heart and comforts my soul.

Soothes my racing mind.

He's limp and lumpy, but full of grace.

Sitting silently on my bed.

Quietly waiting for when

I need him next.

My pink and white pal.

Self Love

When you feel
you don't have enough
time for yourself –
that's when you
really do need
Self Love.
Keep doing
a little something
every day.

How I Saved Myself

Not for me but for mine
Or so I thought
I found the strength
By looking back.
Back to my childhood
Spent in silence.
Intuition, instinct strong.
That's THE truth.
Not the words of others, blind.
Blind by convention, by
Authority, by fear.
When I fly free the whispering
Wind drowns out their words.
Like arrows they falter and drop
Whilst I fly strong and sure.
My world sustains me,
Feeds me and strengthens
Me more.
Finally, it is my voice that I can hear
in the whispering wind.
My voice, reassuring and calm.
My voice that got me through.
Got me here.
My voice that guides mine,
To listen to their own voices.
Their own instinct, their own intuition.

Letter to Yourself in 5 Years

To Future Self,

Well done! Go, Goddess, Go! Celebrate and express! Remember to show gratitude for all you've accomplished: remember how you've overcome your fears and loss of courage... celebrate it!

The tools Joy gave you to move forward, are your tools for life. Your instinct is always true, your passion for life undimmed. Fear is a weapon imposed upon you, but only if you allow it.

When you feel lost, remember what you learnt and how this will pass. It is momentary and you have the power to change how you feel.

Illustration by Nash

"GO, GODDESS, GO!"

My Journey to JOY

I began my journey in JOY with a lovely lady who helped and supported me along the way. She became very inspiring and was a role model of how I aspired to be. She had experienced both good and bad, so was able to empathise with me. Allowing me to learn how to cope with both good and bad times in my own life. She has influenced me in such a positive way and made me who I am today. She continues to support me. I have become an Enhanced Peer Mentor for the JOY Project and my journey is not over yet.

Disney Princes and Fairytale Endings

Growing up we are read fairytales where the lady is rescued or saved by the male. It is really hard in this current society to see the man as a hero. These tales are based on old-fashioned views, where a man is portrayed as the love of a woman's life.

In my life, I have been in a failed marriage and then had two domestic abuse relationships. I have had to learn how to cope and how to recognise the signs of abuse. I've learnt to put my head and heart into gear. You need to trust your gut instinct.

As for Princes... I need to get to know a man first before I would ever sleep with them. I'm not keen on dating sites and find them very untrustworthy.

I need to meet a real man who is kind, considerate and caring not abusive, controlling or demanding. I want to make my own decisions and decide who I spend my time with.

My Thank You to DAWN

I was introduced to the DAWN Project in February 2019.
When I first attended, I joined the Freedom Programme.
Initially, I was unable to speak to the other women in the
group, so I just sat quietly and observed. I went every
week on a Thursday, and also went to one-on-one sessions
with a support worker.

Over time, I opened up. I met other women in the same
situation as myself, and I got a lot of support from
attending this group. They improved my confidence
and helped me to go outside and meet other people.
We had a rule that we were not allowed to speak to one
another outside of the group, as anyone could still be in a
domestic abuse relationship.

I am still in contact with the DAWN Project and offer
support to women in the same situation as myself. I am a
caring person who really wants to give something back.

I Am A Diamond

I am pink. I am girly and I radiate kindness, love and helping other people.

I am a freesia. Beautiful, with a gorgeous scent, brightening up your day.

I am like a dog. Loyal, great company. I don't answer back. I enjoy fresh air and going for walks, it helps me to forget my troubles and meet people.

I am a diamond. Precious, sparkly and bright. I catch the light and twinkle, like a shining star.

I am from Newcastle on Tyne. The place I was born. I love Geordies, they are wonderful, friendly people with a great sense of humour. I love driving into Newcastle, past the Angel of the North or over the Tyne Bridge. Whey Aye Man!

I enjoy walking along the beach on a bright, summer day, with the waves splashing over my feet. The sun hot on my face, the feeling of wellbeing.

I love to sit under a willow tree. Nice and relaxing, hidden from view, enjoying my own company and space.

The summer makes me feel good. I love the warmth on my face, making me feel relaxed and able to reflect. I love sipping a glass of wine with a friend on a hot summer's day.

I love to watch woodpeckers. Their vibrant colours, the special way they peck the tree to gain food. They are very kind and look after their young well.

Rising in the morning, I love relaxing with a nice cup of tea, reflecting on the day and activities ahead.

Treasured Object

My Mum gave me a locket that my Dad had purchased for her. It was the first gift my Dad had bought for my Mum, aged 18 years. It has a lot of sentimental value, and people always comment on it. The locket is heart shaped and opens to allow me to put a photograph of my parents inside. It has a different pattern on either side, so can be worn two different ways. I am eternally grateful to my Mum for giving me such a sentimental gift. This is even more pertinent, as my ex partner stole all of my jewellery.

Me in Five Years

To Future Self,

I will be free from investigations and have justice, I will be able to move on with my life.

I will be more relaxed and will have recommenced my career.

I will have my registration back as a nurse and will be more sympathetic and understanding to those who have been through similar things as me.

I will have a clear DBS certificate.

My ex will be in prison for wasting police time.

I will finally be able to move on with my life.

I will make the time to relax and maintain me time.

I will make something of myself.

I will move to a nice area and have nice friends and family around me.

I owe so much to my Mum who will be 88 years old and has supported me throughout this horrendous experience.

Illustration by Cassie

"I AM **FINALLY** ABLE TO MOVE ON WITH MY **LIFE**"

Sunflower

I am orange.
Colourful, bright, brave.
Fire in my belly. Ready to shine.

I am sunflower
Standing tall and
Strong.

I am a lion.
Full of courage.
Ready to roar.

I am rose quartz.
Healing
My life.

I am home.
A safe haven.
A place I can be me.

I am an ocean.
I feel powerful.
I am ready to dive in and
Wash away the past.

I am an oak tree.
Feeling stronger with each year.
Growing more powerful
Every season.

I am spring.
Full of colour, coming alive again.
Waking up after a dark winter.
There's light in my life again.

I am a bird of prey.
On a mountain, feeling strong.
I have my wings.
I am ready to fly high.

I am dawn.
Watching the sun set.
Feeling alive with the new day.
My chance to start again.

You

You tried to break me

You stole my confidence

But I defied you and continued to rise

You kept me down with your nasty words

You beat me

You turned my home into a prison

You controlled me

You saw me as a puppet

You used my strings to get me to dance

To your own tune

You thought you had won

You didn't think I would fight back

But I did

I rose like the sun

I banished the dark

I let the light in

I cut those strings

I took the power back

I was brave

I was like a butterfly

who found her wings

I now fly free from you

"I ROSE LIKE THE SUN... I LET THE LIGHT IN"

My Story

As a teenager, I had no confidence and low self-esteem. I didn't have many friends and I was bullied for many years. I was always dreaming of a better life, a life of happiness. I spent so much time dreaming about being rescued by a man. As a teenager that was my ambition in life, to find my Prince Charming. The Disney films gave me hope to cling on to, if Cinderella could find her happy ending, then so could I.

I lost myself in the world of Jane Austen. Mr Darcy was my first love. So, I waited for my Fairy Godmother to arrive to do her magic and send my prince to me.

In the end, I was rescued. It took me a long time to realise the only person who was going to recue me, was me. I was my own Fairy Godmother. I had the power to change my own life around. Unfortunately, it took me half my life to realise this.

By the time I was 21, I was getting desperate. Prince Charming still hadn't knocked down my bedroom door and taken me away from my unhappy existence. On my 21st birthday, I went through a very traumatic experience which left me very vulnerable.

A few months after, I went out with friends. I was looking forward to my evening out. I had no idea that this innocent night would change my life, and not in a good way. Over the years I have often wished that I had a time machine, and could travel back to that night and beg myself to stay in instead.

That was the night my ex came into my life. I was very drunk – in those days I used alcohol to make me feel more confident. When he came over to me and asked to buy me a drink, I was very grateful that he was paying me attention.

After that night things happened very quickly, we were in a relationship within a few days and living together within a few months. I was so desperate to have a boyfriend I ended up with the first man who showed an interest in me.

I wanted Prince Charming; I ended up with his evil twin. Of course, to start with he really was charming and so nice to me, he became my whole life. We weren't able to have children. It was just the two of us. I became very isolated.

Eventually, I realised that I didn't love him. I fell in love with a lie, with who he pretended to be. By the time I realised this, it was too late. I couldn't leave. I was trapped.

Over the next few decades, this man, mentally, physically and sexually abused me. He had complete control over me. Over the years I wanted to leave, but I didn't know how to. I think part of me was scared to be on my own, and I was so dependent on him. I got to the point where I felt I deserved it. When someone tells you most days you are not good enough, you start to believe it. He would hit me, and I would end up apologising to him for making him do it. That's how low I got.

In the beginning, there were good times. He did just enough for me to stay. The last five years of our relationship were the worst. By this point, I thought I would never leave him. He thought he had all the control and the power.

Then my life changed again. This time for the better. I finally did it. I ended the relationship. That day we had an argument. He ended up attacking me, he hit me and put his hands around my neck. It wasn't the first time, but this time it felt different. It was the worst I had seen him. I felt he was capable of killing me.

Eventually, he left the flat to get alcohol. I was really scared of what would happen when he got back. In that moment I realised that I deserved so much better. I did the hardest, bravest thing I have ever done. I phoned the police. The police were great with me, they helped me get my life back.

The following months weren't easy, because he wouldn't leave me alone. He ended up in prison for breaking the restraining order. But I was still free from him, for the first time in my life I wasn't having to walk on eggshells. I didn't have to live my life in fear anymore.

For me, the first lockdown came at the right time. It gave me the time to breathe again. To work on me. It was hard at first. I started again from scratch. I was like a child who had been given a blank canvas and an endless supply of colourful paints. I had so much fun filling in that canvas. I have colour back in my life, after so many years of being in the dark.

It's been over three years now and my life has changed so much. I have some really good friends. I have rediscovered my love of music, rock music has become a passion of mine. I go to a lot of gigs, it has helped me to heal, to get through the difficult times.

The one thing that has helped me a lot is being part of the JOY Project. It is a project for women, when I first went to JOY I was a mess. I had only been out of my relationship for a few weeks. When I walked through those doors I had no idea of what to expect. It turned out to be one of the best things I did.

For the first few weeks I just sat there not talking to anyone, but that was ok. There was no pressure for me to do anything. I had finally found a safe place, a place where I could be me. Where no one judged me. These days I don't just sit there quietly, I have my voice back.

The JOY Project and the DAWN Project have given me the tools to rebuild my life. They have helped me to realise that what I went through wasn't my fault. I'm very grateful that I had the strength to walk through that door that day. I'm starting to get my identity back.

These days I'm not looking for Prince Charming. I'm happy being single. I'm working on my relationship with myself. I'm my own superhero.

I will be honest. It hasn't always been easy. I still have bad days where I have flashbacks, but I am strong. I won't let the bad memories of the past hold me back. Despite the bad days, leaving him was the best thing I ever did. This is my story, my journey. I'm just at the beginning. I have so much more to look forward to. I have finally found my wings. I'm ready to fly high and fly free.

The Tower

In my tower, waiting
To be rescued
The door is locked
Where is my Prince Charming?
I know he is coming
He has the key
To the tower door
To get me out
To save me
He must come
Life is so dark right now
But it's ok
He will be here soon
On his horse
To take me away
From this hell
He will come
I have to cling to that belief
That's what gets me
Through the days
Each day I ask myself
Where is he?
I can't live like this
I need to be rescued
The years go by
I'm still in my tower
Still waiting
He hasn't arrived
But he must be close

But wait
What if he doesn't exist?
What if he is just an illusion?
A fairytale.
A lie that Disney
Has been telling us
Since childhood
He's not coming
But I still need
To be rescued
But by who?
Suddenly, everything
Becomes clear
There is only one person
Who can rescue me
ME!
I go to the tower door
I take a deep breath
I pull the handle
It's not locked
It never was
It was my fear
That kept it locked
I'm ready
To rescue myself
To walk through the door
To be free

"I HAVE **FINALLY** FOUND MY **WINGS**"

My Light Bulb Moment

Living in the dark for

So long

Having no voice

There's no way out

I'm trapped

I'm not brave enough

To break free of

The chains that keep

Me in this prison

Each day is about

Surviving

Trying not to anger

My jailer

There's no point of dreaming

Of a better life

There's no light at

The end of the tunnel

But then one day

Things changed

I suddenly see things

Clearly

I finally have my light bulb moment

I'm ready to break

Free

Enough is enough

I'm not scared anymore

It's been a long journey

But finally I can

See the light at

The end of the

Tunnel

I'm ready to walk

Towards the light

Advice for anyone still in a bad situation

When I first left him, people used to ask me 'why didn't you leave him sooner?' I used to hate that question. Leaving is not that easy! That lie was all I knew, I spent most of my adult life with him.

We stay for all kinds of reasons. For me, I felt I didn't deserve better. I was scared to leave. I was so dependent on him, I had no idea how to live independently.

If you are reading this and you feel you're not ready to leave right now... that's ok. I know how hard it is. Just be kind to yourself. Start taking tiny steps now, work on yourself, build up your confidence. Make a plan. There will be a time when you will have a light bulb moment, and you will be ready to change your life.

When you do leave, have a safety plan. I didn't have a plan, I just told him I was ending the relationship, he went crazy. I was in fear for my life. Make a plan, phone the police or Women's Aid or the DAWN Project. Stay safe.

IF you are reading this and feel ready, but are overwhelmed and have no idea what to do. Break everything up into small steps. Try not to look at the big picture. Just take that first step, that first step changes your life.

My first step was phoning the police and asking for help. Then I took another step and another, those steps transformed my life.

You are enough, you deserve better, you can do this. You are stronger than you think! Take those steps, you will soon see that beautiful light at the end of the tunnel.

Turning My Life Around

Turning home from a place of danger to a safe place

Turning sadness into laughter

Turning a prison into freedom

Turning tears into joy

Turning the gloomy dark rooms into a burst of vibrant colour

Turning the darkness into light

Turning a building into a home

Turning feeling trapped into hope

Turning a nightmare into my dreams

Turning my silence into a voice

A voice ready to help others

Turn their living hell into a life worth living

Strength

Your strength has

Got you this far

Through the dark days

Has kept you safe

You've had the strength of a lion

The fire of a dragon

You held your head up high

You faced the dark days

Even though you were living in fear

You faced the world when

Everyone was talking about you

You roared when all you

Really wanted to do was

Whimper and hide

Now you are safe

It's ok not to feel strong

It can be tiring

Having to always be strong

Let the unshed tears come

Let it out

Rest

Just sit with it

You don't have to keep

Fighting

Pushing yourself

Take time out

Read

Listen to music

Just be

And take comfort in

Knowing

That when you need

It your fire and strength

Will always be there for you

But just for now

Relax

And rest

Breathe

Everything is going to be ok

Brave

Be brave

Let go of the fear

Have faith

Step out of the dark

Walk towards the light

Let go of the past

Live in the moment

Laugh

Smile

Love

Let yourself be happy

Forgive

Break free of your chains

Nourish your soul and body

Don't justify yourself to anyone

Be your own superhero

Hold your head up high

Dance in the rain

Sing

Always be at your best

Roar

Have fire in your belly

Surround yourself

With positive people

Let negative feelings dissolve

Be your own cheerleader

Be kind

Shine in and out

Be real

Take risks

Dream

Believe

Look at the stars

When overwhelmed –

Rest for a while

Be still

Breathe

Then dust yourself off

Stand tall

Open the door

Walk towards your dreams

A step at a time

Enjoy the journey

Keep moving forward

Believe in miracles

Magic and

Fairy dust

Mantras

The positive thoughts you have today and the positive decisions and choices you make today will create the happy amazing future you deserve.

If you are looking for someone to change your life, to rescue you... look in the mirror. You are the only one who can change your life.

My Power

I am a woman with power.

A superhero.

A woman with the power to change things.

The power to turn the darkness into light.

To turn my dreams into reality.

To turn the ashes of the past into hope for the future.

To turn the silence into a voice

loud enough to help others find their power.

I've always had this power,

But for so long I was afraid to use it –

So, I kept it hidden away.

Now, I let it out.

I can feel the power within me.

The power shining.

I will never let it dim again.

I Was...

I was lost.

I was broken.

I was scared.

I was still clinging to the past.

I had no voice.

No identity.

I was alone in the world.

Too scared to trust anyone.

I wanted to run away, to hide

But I managed to find the strength

To open the door and

Walk into Joy.

To start my journey,

To rediscover me again,

To be free.

I Am...

I am strong.

I am powerful.

I am in control.

I am moving forward.

I am in the driving seat.

For so many years,

I was a passenger in my own life.

Letting others control me,

But now I've taken the steering wheel back.

There may be times when I get lost,

Or take the wrong path,

Or even crash.

But that's ok.

I can just take a different direction.

Make a different choice.

I hold the steering wheel to my life.

I am in control.

I am ready to shine.

I am in control.

I have a voice.

Dear Future Self

Keep going.

Keep moving.

It's ok to go slow.

Be kind to yourself.

Stay strong.

Be brave.

Don't get frustrated because you're

Not where you want to be right now.

All of your small steps,

Will soon add up.

You are so close to being the you

Who you are meant to be.

Keep planting your seeds of hope.

Water those seeds daily.

Be patient.

Like those seeds you will slowly start to grow,

To flourish,

To shine.

Your future will be a garden,

Full of beautiful sunflowers.

A future full of light and colour.

In the meantime, just enjoy the journey,

Towards the amazing future that you deserve.

"YOUR **FUTURE** WILL BE A **GARDEN,** FULL OF **BEAUTIFUL SUNFLOWERS"**

Illustration by Michelle

"THERE'S **MORE** TO **ME,** THAN MY **STORY"**

Hope

I am not who I used to be,
I hope and strive to be again,
But this time round a stronger, happier version,
One who feels absolutely free.

Every day when I awake,
I look up at the sky and feel grateful to be alive,
My battlewounds are invisible and unknown to the world,
But I know they are my driving force for striving –
Every day to be happy and free.

Safe

I see my nestling spot; and my heartbeat slows so I feel that relief of knowing that once sat – enveloped by the comfort and colours – I am safe.

From my little self-made nest... the sight and activity of blue tits, hedge sparrows, turtle doves, the robin – so bold! Then, my favourite, Mr. Tom – I hear his beautiful song and it lifts me... then he appears, proudly serenading me – or so I like to think – from his orange berry encrusted tree throne. He is our Mr. Tom – blackbirds never leave their place.

I look up at the sky, so blue with ever changing white fantastical creatures drifting ethereal across the sun. Or be it dark, dangerous and moody – the drama and anticipation of a storm. But I am safe from any storm in my nest of rainbows, mirrors, crystals and silks... soft velour and snuggly, tasselly coverings. My one place where I feel that I am me, with my thoughts and feelings. Reading, talking to my cats, my offspring, myself!

Taking time out in peace without peopling is what I seek!

Grateful

To be safe and not fearful in my own little house...

To hold my children just for the love and joy and not for protection...

For throwing on scruffs, woolies and wellies, grabbing some snacks and walking out the front door to go for a big stomp up the cow fields and hill meadows with the kids... enjoying the fresh air and trees... the amazing view. Knowing we will walk back down the hill to home... with dinner in the oven, ready to warm us. Comfort us.

I am grateful for the stars and moon when I look up at night... the magic and awe as my eyes adjust and I see more...

To be able to come to Horizon again and to be part of this inspiring group that has given me confidence in my ability to still write. And to feel accepted. Not alone.

The Epiphany

In the minutes of quiet contemplation; following my unbreakable vow, promise (never broken to a child), to my Bebe that she could have a baby girl bunny off her friend; my mind spiralled down its very own rabbit-hole.

Memory. Buried like soil. A death of my past... resurrected.

I, Me, I remembered house rabbits, bunnies! My furry, lop-eared, bouncy, cuddly, naughty, beautiful babies...

The pure joy of their long, soft, flappy-face-muffs!

Thuddy, almost armlike, cashmere feet...

Chocolate-melt eyes that could make you give in to any demand or threat...

Suddenly. Sadness. Shock. Realisation. I will change this for her, for her Bebe.

HE TOOK MY LOVE.

HE GOT MY BUNNY.

I begged and pleaded and was made to feel like HE was doing a nice thing.

THEN once, I, me in love with my new baby. HE began the slow withdrawal. CRUELLY... taking it away, bit by bit. Changing the rules of where, how it could be, feed, sleep... all decisions out of my power. HE saw my pain.
HE saw the worry, Anxiety. Suffering. THEN BLAMED ME! My fault.

He did it with every child, animal, pet, hobby, friend...

NOW I SEE.

We, Bebe and I are going to get a baby girl house bunny and there will be total joy (and fur!)

Epiphany 2

Single Mother.

Go on! Say it...

Worthless. Never going to be able to provide or care for her children, NEEDY. SAD.

BROKEN.

I found strength I never knew existed... a strength I had harnessed from the years of hurt. Harm, hate, neglect, fear, hunger and survival.

My babies, no matter how old they are or become, are my breath.

That is being a Single Mother.

There is a stigma ingrained in the psyche of all humans that tells us that women are less.

Women are unable.

Women need men.

Women need help.

Women are here to make life easier for others.

Well, that is the lie that others that need women tell themselves.

Women are the cogs of our universe.

I am a Single Mother.

It happened.

I chose to live

And to give my babies life.

Not merely survival.

"I FOUND **STRENGTH** I NEVER KNEW **EXISTED"**

"YOU'RE **ONE** OF **US**"

I Rise

I rise with my young wisdom.

I rise from the air of salt, pepper and cinnamon.

A storm of light.

Sounds of thunder and lightning.

To wash everything away, for another regrowth.

I rise with all the elements under my feet,

And wrapped around me.

I rise knowing I have peace and

New homes, in DAWN and JOY.

Refuge

I had to leave
My home
My town
My life
I lived in a refuge in a new place.
With clothes on my back and nothing more.
My son who was with me was only three.
I was nervous and scared, I felt alone.
But...
Other women were there with me.
They understood.
Our kids played together.
They gave me understanding and hope.
Things didn't have to be said out loud,
We just understood one another.
This strange new place
Was where I found kindness and support.
We all bonded, we helped each other and
 taught one another new things.
From the simplest task to the most confusing,
We had each other.
It meant that this place, was not a home,
But it was a step in knowing that we weren't alone.
We laughed, we cried and we got mad.
We did it all together.
We are sisters.

Always My Story?

What happened doesn't mean that's it.

It's more like one chapter in a whole book.

Is it a good chapter? A bad one?

A mix of emotions?

It's just a set of emotions, from a time.

Some I learned as a child, some growing up.

I have a new set of emotions now.

It's not just one way or another.

The same as my "story"

There's more to me,

Than my story, than one chapter.

Who Will Save You?

You! You'll have this little switch that will go off. It's time, time to go, to say, to leave.

That dull feeling will become a sacred and nervous one, heart racing, weird feelings but that switch has been turned, you can do this.

Ignore the bad vibes, those who don't believe you. Hold your head high and start your new chapter.

Eye contact is difficult to start with. Talking out loud is hard. You're nervous and shaking and making yourself feel small.

It all still counts. They see you, they support you.

That new chapter will possibly be a huge blur. So many changes and places. But you did it! You! No one else saved you.

A day you'll never forget – you'll hate that day, but give it time and you'll see it as the first step of freedom that you made.

Who Am I?

I don't know who I am. Me, myself and I.

I am who I am with different people. New people, people close to me and strangers.

I am someone who doesn't have to tell you!

Trinket Box

Old, white, silver ribboned,

soft pearls, small, decorated patterns.

Lift the lid to the first rose we plucked,

Sleeping inside.

I kept it safe,

For as long as I could.

I look and look,

Trying to find a replacement,

But I know it wouldn't be the same.

Our hearts were bound to the trinket box,

And even though it's now gone,

It's still in my heart,

Just like you are.

Do We Help Women Only?

No. Female/Male.
LGBTQIA+

I'm cupi, bisexual, ace!
I was treated and spoken to just like anyone else.
NO JUDGEMENT!
We're all the same.

Go by they/their/them?
Cool!

Identify as male or female?
Proud of you!

Go by neither?
Love you, for you.

We see you as you are,
You're one of us!

I Am The Hills

I am yellow, stand out

From the rest.

I am orchid, tall

And colourful.

I am a ferret, Cheeky, weird

Full of mischief and funny moments.

I am the hills, full of personality

And unknowns.

I am a zebra tree. Standing

Out, being unique.

I am autumn. Feelings changing.

Colours becoming new and fresh,

Enjoying the crisp air.

I am a dinosaur who learns

What's in front of me and around me.

Learning from a pink dinosaur!

I am bedtime. Ready to rest

And just enjoy the smells and sounds.

DAWN

The first place, where I was believed.

Where I was understood.

They let me cry, to feel emotion.

They made me feel real.

They were there the whole time,

And at my pace.

They held my hand and

Made me feel safe.

For the first time, I felt seen, protected

And in a place where I belonged.

I will never forget them,

Or go too far from them.

They supported me,

And now I support them too.

DAWN, is the place that saved me.

"I AM A WOMAN WITH POWER"

Police

Wrapped in warmth, kindness, gentle words and kind expressions.

The feeling of being safe, cared for, seen.

Protected. From early morning until late at night.

Always there, right until the end.

Until you could do no more.

Thank you, Officer AB.

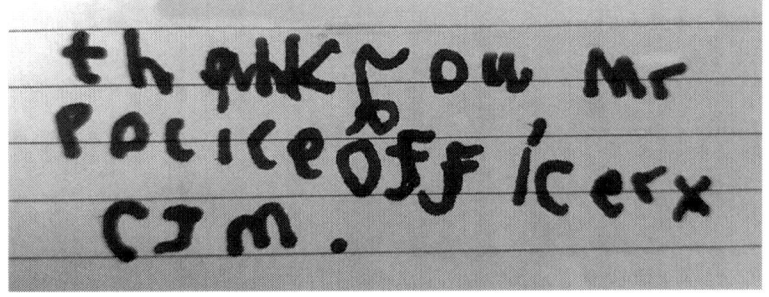

A's son, age 7

Seed, Growing, Blooming (for Louise)

Blooming and growing

Every year finding more

About the real me

With others: seed, grow and

Bloom with me.

Little Feet

Little feet learning to
Walk on eggshells
Painful, sore and red
Petals under

Faces on posters in the
Dark, scary, watching on.
Cold room, feels big until
Bed sharing. It'll be morning soon.

Egg shells are now a dance floor,
Lights hiding soft areas. Dance
From light to light.
Ouch! Fake light.
Little rose petals.

Lack feeling feet or just
A part of life.

Stone walls, stone floors,
Wood holding up life
Hurts more than egg shells
But the longer it is the harder
To sleep on the stone floor.

Walk room to room, long
Loose hairs running when
Walked passed.
Nothing happened
As I touch the small
Spots on my hand.

Solid plug sockets unused
Unless a forceful push,
Hits a soft spot or two
Each time.

The mind is a whirlwind
Or in the deep snow
Fuzzy confused.
Random strangers offering pills
I am crazy.

Why is life so hard to take?
Thigh scars, arm scars.
Little ones from
Going crazy
Still here.

Sat on the side looking
Out of the window.
My stunning cat jumps
Up purring.
We give each other cuddles
Both with multicoloured skin.

Buttons

White with brown spots.
Buttons the hamster.

Little secret place with him
Safe, kind, loved
Little shadow, ever so clever.
My whole heart/best friend
X

Never judge an animal as
All love and care.

A New Stage in My Life

I Was...

I was in the cold-faced, unknown stage of walls up. Interested in nothing. Feelings off. I thought that was the normal way to be. I gave attitude, I wouldn't respond. I was always up for a fight. Care for no one, always on the lookout. Befriend no one, trust no one.

Two years on...

Defrosted heart, open to new things and things I've found interesting, fun or different. It isn't difficult to trust anymore. Not with the tools that JOY taught me. Helping others in now something that I enjoy. My quirkiness isn't weird. My mental health isn't anything to be hidden or embarrassed about. I have people I talk to without shutting down. I have support, help and friends. I support and help others. I'm at a new stage in my life. A stage of being the new, real me. I enjoy the seasons, with no regrets.

To The Future Me...

Have we celebrated things? Christmas, Easter, birthdays? Seen fireworks?

Slept outside in the woods?

Forgiven and fully moved on?

We (me, myself and I) have been through so much from the age of four, it's time for us to live our best life now. Explore all the things we secretly like.

Today... we are a survivor.

Now... we are a warrior.

Always love, be free, be happy and laugh at ourselves.

Be humble, but never forget.

Keep standing in the rain, watch it all wash away,

See the new growth.

"FREEDOM AT LAST"

Happiness

The pit is comfortable, and I am content

But am I?

There may be exciting things on the outside

Perhaps if I climb out, I could be part of them.

But should I?

Am I happy, or simply complacent?

Unless I make the effort and climb out

I will never know.

Time

Time never stands still.

A second is gone as soon as you are aware of it.

Why does time 'fly' or never end?

You can have a happy time or a bad time and even no time.

But where is time when you need it?

Time is here – in the moment.

Make the most of it, as it doesn't last for ever.

Freedom (Being 70!)

Freedom at last!

Not answerable to anyone.

Can do as I like.

I'm old (70!) and glad to be.

Not judged by my looks.

Excused for being a bit batty and forgetful.

Life's pleasures are free – naps, sunshine, walking barefoot in the grass or through the waves, listening to music, reading, writing, painting, gardening, singing, being with family/friends...

What more could anyone want?

The Dance is Over

My partner in the dance
Doesn't give me a chance
I hold him very tight
He says: "That's not right"
So, I let him go...
and that's... so-so.

I read the books
I seek advice
and try again, being extra nice.
I try and try, but it's still no good.
My good intentions are misunderstood.

The blame was mine
But not this time.
It takes two to Tan go
It cannot be done so lo

Finally... The dance is over.

Games People Play

– The Boss sets the rules but doesn't tell anyone what they are.

– If the rules are broken then a penalty is given, i.e., the Player does not get told what they have done, as they are expected to 'read the Boss's mind'.

– The Boss then sulks and acts like a naughty child and throws a tantrum – shouting, swearing; banging and making a noise; he doesn't clean up after doing tasks or clear things away. He leaves a mess everywhere and switches the lights off as he leaves the room.

The Player has no choice but to accept the Boss's behavior and do whatever possible to please the Boss and do whatever he wants.

The Boss then starts being nice to the Player by behaving like a person who cares and wants the Player to be happy.

The Player is lulled into a false sense of security for a while, but the wheel continues going round.

Stop the Clock

Stop the clock; my life's on hold.

But I'm running out of time.

There simply aren't enough hours in the day

To be myself, feed myself, look after myself and pay the bills; shop; clean, etc etc.

I'm running out of time

But I 'feel the fear and do it anyway'

My goal is in sight. Freedom is on the horizon.

But please stop the clock as my muddled brain can't cope for much longer... I need more time!

"It's too late now"

Little did I know when I met Prince Charming (when I was 21) that he would turn out to be a devil in disguise.

I fell in love with him on our first date and I thought that he loved me too and maybe he did, but he never expressed it. He never told me he loved me. When I asked him why he didn't show me any love, he replied "What is love?"

I asked him to tell me what he did like and he said (in priority order): "No. 1 – football; No 2 – sex; No 3 – me."

Control

I'm Rita and Shirley rolled into one. With a bit of a Dagenham Girl, plus a chain maker too.

They fought for their right to be who they were – something I didn't do.

I let someone else take control of my life – expecting me to be a dutiful housewife.

I knew exactly what to do, but didn't do anything except write reams of notes about being abused. When all he wanted was for me to be happy.

He did his best to provide for the family by working hard and earning money to pay for our food. Plus, he dealt with maintenance tasks.

Deep down... he's a good man, but he went down the wrong path.

The World of Never Never

The sun has gone down

And it's a warm, still evening.

I listen to the sounds of the birds singing; the bees buzzing

(and the lorries roaring)

The moon has risen and there is a soft pink glow in the sky.

As I watch the birds soaring overhead

And gently stroke the dog on my lap

I am aware of the beauty surrounding me

What a shame someone is calling me to go inside for tea

I want this feeling to last forever

But that only happens in 'the world of never-never'

How to Find Happiness

We struggle with life, looking for 'happiness'
When, what we need to do, is stop searching and just 'be'.

But... how?

Listen to the wind
Listen to the sea

Look at things around you...
Really, really, see.

Feel the warmth of the sun
The smoothness of a stone

Feel the beauty of living
And the joy of giving.

Think not of yourself and your needs
Think of the pain & suffering of others.
Give them your time and energy
And in them, sow the seeds

Only then, when you do not seek happiness for yourself,
will you find it.

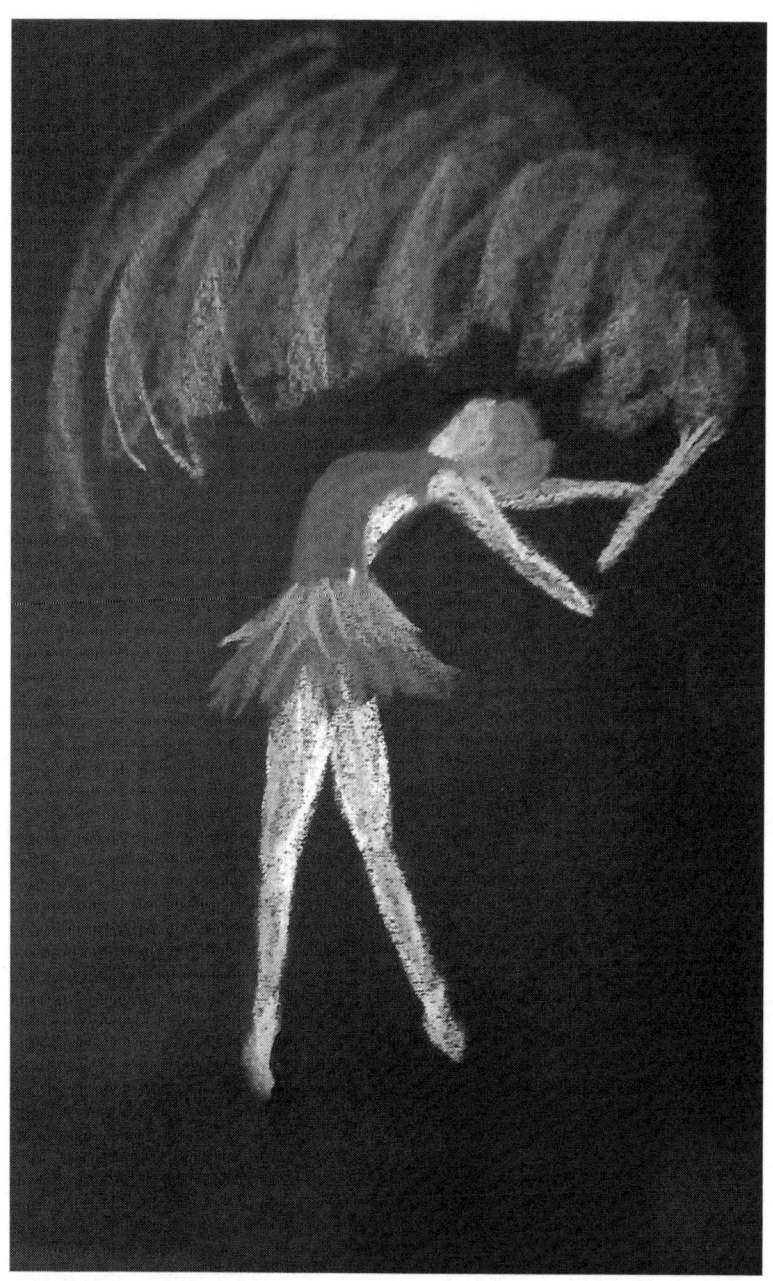

Illustration by Michelle

"I AM DETERMINED. I AM **ME**"

Self

Dear Self,

Despite all your troubles, please remember how far you have come. Others are seeing you do well. You're on the right path. You may not see it, but you are. No matter how hard things are, remember how many times you got back, yes you, you got back up.

You are strong, you are positive. Don't let negativity dim your light.

You're creative, you're colourful.

Most of all, listen to those around you... you are a good mum, you are a good person.

You can love yourself, it's not selfish. Those who think you are, don't listen. You are not like them. You need to help and support yourself so that you don't burn out and become poorly.

You've got this!

Yours faithfully and sincerely,

Self.

A Treasured Item

I don't really have a particular treasured item, for I treasure more than one. Most of my treasures are from close friends and family. Anything from my first ever teddy, Brian, to a Christmas card from my Nan. There are also things that I've worked hard for. They remind me how hard I worked, the dedication that I never gave up. A special treasure to hold light or even pass on for luck.

I Rise

Every time I am struggling

or knocked

down

I rise

for I am a woman with power

I am me

I won't give up

I rise every morning, for I am

a woman with

power

I am determined. I am

me.

Some days, some moments

in time may be hard

or difficult

but despite all these set backs

It's ok. I rise.

No matter what.

A letter of thanks to JOY

Dear JOY Project,

Beginning the JOY Project, back in 2019, I was scared and nervous not knowing what to expect, who I would be meeting or even what I was doing.

I went through one of the world's biggest crises (lockdown) together with the JOY Project. The gratitude I have... there are no words.

I want to say a huge thank you. I met some amazing women who I worked alongside, sharing stories and experiences.

After it was safe and lockdown had lifted, it was a true blessing to meet these ladies in person.

I felt my confidence grow and grow.

You would help and guide me. You'd say that it was all me putting the work in, but it was your guidance that helped me to finally set goals in my life. Before, I was lost with no ideas, just lost.

Thank you and much gratitude.

"I AM **IMPORTANT.** EVERY **ONE** OF US IS"

My Story

Life has taken a few very difficult turns. So much so that without the help I needed I don't believe I would have gotten through. At times I felt I had to scream out for help, as asking felt ignored.

So, I had to feel so much pain before I got there, but I finally have the support I need.

The day I decided enough was enough with my relationship, the end of 2018. I struggled to find somewhere to live (as I already had a mortgage with my ex) I struggled to get stability for myself and the children.

After I found a flat and moved out, I started to rebuild myself. After being used to have children. After being ignored, being belittled and gaslighted. I felt incapable, wrong and stupid. I started claiming CM, CB and UC and everything I needed to create stability, painted the flat and built a home. I started to believe in myself again.

The day my life was turned upside down again was in 2020. This destroyed me. I remember the air; how cloudy it was and how the crows seemed to know something I didn't as they swooped so close.

Before that, the goalposts kept moving every time I thought there was an agreement and I couldn't understand why.

After the court's decision to take the children away for a week or two at a time, to someone who still seemed to act blameless of the way she'd treated me. I remember how calm she was when she saw me collapsed and devastated at the loss. She looked emotionless and so put together. To me, it was a sum up of what our relationship meant to her. Nothing. She looked empty.

After that day, I gained weight and felt like my emotions were on a constant rollercoaster from week to week which felt impossible to maintain.

I had lost my stability in income, the CM, CB and some of the UC, needing to justify why I needed this money and that I was the mother to both children as UC could only find a record of one. Everything felt unstable, the routine for my job, my income, my mental health and the people that made the decision still seemed blameless. I still fought, and with the help of the DAWN programme I worked through to freedom. I learnt to recognise behaviours. With the help of my colleagues, I appealed. Representing myself through lack of funds. I appealed the CM decision and the CB decision. I tried with every fibre of my being to create stability, until I had nothing left.

I kept in touch with the doctors and started taking medication, which impacted my ability to work and left me feeling fuzzy – like I was watching a film, instead of taking part in my own life.

I kept thinking that these magistrates deciding that taking children away from their mother (who had been there for them since birth) for a week at a time, was fair.

They were wrong!

But that doesn't matter now. She doesn't matter, and the magistrates don't matter. My children had turned into pawns in a twisted game. My mental health suffered. After building my confidence, I seemed to slip away like sand through the gaps in a hand. I felt unworthy to be considered and I wanted to scream.

Nevertheless, everything I said at the time seemed to fall on deaf ears. Until the DAWN project and JOY.

I MATTER too! But I'm not sure I believed it back then.

I felt the need to walk up to people and ask...

Do you see me?

Am I real?

After starting DAWN and JOY, I allowed myself to be open to anything. What helped a great deal was hearing other people's stories and stresses, and feeling an affinity with them. I didn't feel alone.

With DAWN I also completed the Freedom Programme and 'my time' developed into time as a community, and understanding others.

With JOY I truly started to rebuild. Here, it was not about anyone else but me and what I needed. Shifting the focus helped with whatever label was put on the relationship and my ex-partner's behaviour. What happened was not right or fair, and what she did was not right or fair.

JOY opened the doors to me to try creative therapy, the Being Free course. I was able to join a community and be heard.

I felt like I was able to heal my cracked soul – with much stronger stuff. I relearnt stuff that I thought I knew, but there's knowing and really knowing!

I learnt to understand and respect myself and to forgive myself. To appreciate my own value. I had to take steps to do that, I found that rushing only made me worse. Causing me to break down again.

You can't heal fast. You need to go at a pace your body can handle. I learnt so much.

Thank you, Zahida, JoRae and Kerry for this very important project.

I am important. Every one of us is.

Sometimes, things happen that we can't justify and that are not fair, but it's not a reflection on us.

Sometimes, it has nothing to do with us.

It may seem impossible (and it did for me), but with the right support we can get through.

I have decided to take back my power, because no one can have power over me unless I let them.

"MY **FEELINGS** ARE **VALID**"

The Angel

Walking along the pavement,

Only noticing the gravel beneath my feet,

I scurry to the house that is meant to be home.

Locking the door swiftly and checking it twice
upon entering...

I proceed to deal with the constant demands from tiny
little people

That have no idea.

They see me cry, but they don't know why,

They watch on as I cradle my phone,

Wondering who can help me.

I have no-one to call upon,

I'm scared, lost and lonely.

As I lay in bed, I hear distant sounds of intoxicated
laughter outside,

I rush downstairs and curl up by the front door...

I've locked the door, taped the letter box...

Did I lock the windows?

The tears keep falling.

My body feels weak.

Why am I even here? I ask myself.

My children deserve better,

I tell myself.

The depression is real,

The anxiety is fierce,

And being a victim has destroyed me!

But then... an angel came to guide me,

She reached out and listened,

She reassured me and told me that my feelings are valid.

I'm not weak, I do have a purpose...

And I am a good person.

She offered me opportunities to gain confidence

And to learn and build skills I didn't know I had.

She gave me tools to overcome anxious feelings,

And she was always there to lend an ear...

That angel was called JOY!

So, I would like to finish by saying... Thank you to all the staff and women on the JOY Project and Worcester Community Trust for everything you have done for me and with me.

Illustration by Nash

"FULL OF **STARS** THAT **DANCE** THROUGH MY **POEMS**"

I Am Bushehr

I am orange, the sky of my heart is full of fire and love.

I am a cat, searching for caresses.

I am hard, like rocks fighting against the waves of life.

I am the sea. I love holding the sun rise and sun set inside me.

I am Bushehr, my city. A port that loves the sea ahead.

I am a silent desert, full of stars that dance through my poems.

I am a pine tree, who in the winter of life, tries to stay green.

I am autumn, full of colours that feel my sadness
and happiness.

I am a sparrow, carrying the song of freedom.

I am a white morning after a black night, when I step out
of the sorrow.

Liberty

Close your eyes,
Hug yourself and be free
From the huge sufferings
They do not fit your small heart.
Be free from the fault of wounds
From rough earthquakes of sorrow
That throw you, occasionally
Be free, peaceful and conscientious
Sing with your inner sparrow
Sing at the top of the green fantasy tree
Let your fountain of dreams flutter.

Peace

Tell me about the song of swallows

While they are singing and raining

From the wide sky of silence

In the turbulent sea of our soul

Until they give us peace

No Worries

Let me be peaceful here
Away from worries
Relying on white clouds
Until my dreams shower down

Winter

The snow kisses the soil

Winter is pregnant with Spring

We are sitting on the train of life

And life is turning around

Love

In the Winter of your life

Throw your sadness into the wind

Turn on the fire of love inside

And go to the red land

Where all the people are in love

Imagination

My imagination is limitless,

My feelings are infinite.

I am painting with my whole imagination,

I am writing with all of my existence.

An emotional person,

Whose laughter and tears are the same.

Bad Days

Bad days!
Bad days!
I hear your voice
My oppressed country
Don't cry, don't cry
The dark clouds will go soon
We will see the face of the sun
We will feel its heat – without guns!
Brave women of my land
Tulips will grow from your blood
You're the best sample of sacrifice
You're the best pioneers of freedom
A bird said to me
A dancing bird
The horizon is clear
Bad days will turn
Into best days

Illustration by Nash

Reading Recommendations from the group

The Smart Girls Guide to Self Care – Shahida Arabi

DBTselfhelp.org.uk

POWER: Surviving and Thriving After Narcissistic Abuse – Shahida Arabi

You Can Heal Your Life – Louise L. Hay

The Power of Now –Eckhart Tolle

Living Magically – Gill Edwards

Why Does He Do That?: Inside the Minds of Angry and Controlling Men – Lundy Bancroft

Feel The Fear and Do It Anyway – Susan Jeffers

#feelthefearnaddoitanyway

Break The Silence: A Support Guide for Male Victims of Domestic Abuse – Lee Marks

Contact Details for Local & National Mental Health services

What to do if you need mental health support

If you feel you're having mental or emotional difficulties, there's lots of support out there for you:

speak to your GP, they will be able to talk to you and help you find the right support

get support on the phone, you can call the NHS for free on 111 for non-emergency advice and health questions

What to do if you need mental health support Worcestershire

Worcestershire Wellbeing Hub is an information and signposting service for people over the age of 16 who are experiencing low mood, anxiety or stress, and feel that they would benefit from support from local community providers

website: Worcestershire Wellbeing Hub www.worcestershire. wellbeinghub.org.uk

email whcnhs.wellbeinghub@nhs.net

Telephone 01905 766124

If you or someone you know is in immediate risk of physical harm because of a mental health emergency, phone 999 or visit your local A&E.

NHS Mental Health Crisis Helpline Worcester – 0808 196 9127 (24 hrs a day 365 days a year). Please contact the main switchboard if you can't get through who can direct your call – 01905 763333.

There are Mental health Crisis Teams in most areas of the country – so have your areas number at hand – here is Worcestershire's contact details

Worcestershire Crisis Resolution Team
The Crisis Resolution Team can offer telephone support, advice and

guidance and can be phoned outside of normal working times. Phone 0808 196 9127 Call now The Crisis Resolution Team offer advice, support and at times assessment for those people who are in significant Mental Health Crisis.

NHS support

Website: www.nhs.uk/oneyou/everymindmatters

You can also contact The Samaritans: (They are a talking service you don't have to be in full crisis to contact them)

call 116 123

website: www.samaritans.org   or email: jo@samaritans.org

National mental health services:
You can also find advice and speak to someone about mental health at one of these national organisations:

www.mind.org.uk or call 0300 123 3393

www.sane.org.uk or call 0300 304 7000

www.nopanic.org.uk or call 0844 967 4848

www.qwell.io   online service

The Mix - Support for under 25s   themix.org.uk

giveusashout.org available 24/7 or/ text SHOUT to 85258

The DAWN Project Worcester Community Trust
(Domestic Abuse Working Network for women girls and men)
Wychavon, Malvern Hills and Worcester City   Call: 07341 457923

Email: dawn@worcestercommunitytrust.org.uk

Please be aware that this is NOT a 24 hour helpline and we aim to respond to messages within 48 working hours.

West Mercia Women's Aid aim is to reduce the impact of domestic abuse and violence against women and girls, they provide help support and advice (including male victims) with a 24h hr a day helpline, Worcestershire 0800 9803331

Herefordshire, Shropshire, Telford & Wrekin 0800 783 1359

They also provide advice on how to hide your tracks on the internet. for further information

website: www.westmerciawomensaid.org

WMRSASC (West Mercia Rape & Sexual Assault Support Centre) offers specialist support to the victims of rape and sexual violence. Services are free, confidential and non-judgemental

Emotional Support Line: Call 03456 461188 or www.wmrsasc.org.uk

Male Domestic Abuse Helpline 0800 014 9082, available 24hrs daily.

If you are a survivor of sexual abuse:

The Survivors Trust has over 130 member agencies based in the UK and Ireland which provide specialist support for women, men and children who are survivors of rape, sexual violence or childhood sexual abuse. Email: info@thesurvivorstrust.org 08088 010818

The National Association for People Abused in Childhood is a charity that offers support, advice and guidance to adult survivors of any form of childhood abuse. Phone: 0800 085 3330

If you are having suicidal thoughts, help is available. Please reach out...
National Suicide Prevention Lifeline: 0800-273 Talk UK
MIND Info online: 0300 123 3393 Email: info@mind.org.uk Our Infoline provides an information and signposting service. They are open 9am to 6pm, Monday to Friday (except for bank holidays).
National Suicide Prevention Helpline UK
0800 689 5652 www.spbristol.org/NSPHUK

Campaign Against Living Miserably (CALM)
0800 58 58 58 thecalmzone.net

LGBTQi plus Support Services
Call us on 0345 3 30 30 30 or email helpline@lgbt.foundation
Weekdays – 9am until 9pm
Saturday & Sunday – 10am until 5.30pm

Gender Identity Research & Education Society (GIRES)
gires.org.uk

Support for loneliness

Red Cross support line
Call our free confidential support line on 0808 196 3651

Silverline Helpline:
0800 470 80 90 Call free
The Silver Line Helpline is a free, confidential telephone service just for older people.
We provide friendship, conversation and support 24 hours a day, 7 days a week.

Age UK
0800 169 6565 www.ageuk.org.uk 24hrs 7 days a week

www.mind.org.uk

For Bereavement

WAY – Widowed and Young
www.widowedandyoung.org.uk 0300 201 0051
 Monday - Friday – 9.30am-5:00pm

www.mariecurie.org.uk 0800 090 2309 for bereavement through cancer support is free and available 8am-6pm Monday to Friday, and 11am-5pm on Saturdays.

St Richard's Hospice
www.strichards.org.uk – Worcester Gateway Team 01905 763963.

Self-care is a necessity and not a luxury – full stop.

As well as very joyfully being the Project Manager for JOY, JoRae is also a Women's Wellbeing Consultant, Neurolinguistic & Cognitive Behavioural / Processing for Trauma Coach. She has put together this compilation of techniques which she learned from her teachers and training, and which she successfully uses for both herself and in her bespoke courses.

Self-soothing is part of self-care.

Learning how to do this is a journey and takes time. Look to make just a 1 % change a month to bring about lasting effect on your life and wellbeing. Self-regulation and soothing is key to improved mental and physical wellbeing and we are all about that at the JOY Project!

To follow here are some of the top tips we share in the JOY project – practice one of them once daily for at least seven days. Some will be perfect, and others won't and that's OK – it's a bit like some folk liking Marmite and some really not, all these tools and techniques will resonate with some of you and not others. Try and move past resistance to having a go for at least that week before deciding – and remember to enjoy experimenting!

The simplest techniques are often the most effective and I always recommend practising them when you don't need them, so they are at your fingertips when you do!

Always Start with a breath, it's a great reminder to slow down and stop even if just for a few seconds. Try to observe how you feel rather than being inside the feelings...

So, I invite you to take a good slow deep breath (if you can in through the nose, out through the mouth) and remember anyone with asthma or epilepsy needs to exhale twice as long as they inhale!

The quickest way to start emotionally self-regulating is to simply name colours – look around, and use your inner voice "I can see purple, I can see blue, I can see red, I can see green" etc. When we occupy the inner voice with a task, especially identifying colour – it doesn't have time to think about ruminating or fretting about things future or past.

5,4,3,2,1 – This is a classic Mindfulness exercise which I have shaken up a bit (a method originally developed by Dr Ellen Hendricksen)

Take a good slow deep breath (if you can in through the nose, out through the mouth) and remember anyone with asthma or epilepsy needs to exhale twice as long as they inhale! My invite with this exercise too is that you really concentrate on engaging with each sense as you go through the different sensations, really look at what you see, really feel what you touch etc.. and never worry about the order you do these things in – the important thing is engaging with your senses.

5. Look around you – name five things you can see (try to remember to add in a colour of the object you are looking at!) eg "I can see a green leaf, I can see a brown tree etc"

4. Touch something – you can be anywhere and do this technique, no one is going to realise you are doing it if you are sat on a bus or in a waiting room and you touch a piece of jewellery or your glasses, hair clothing skin etc… again use your inner voice – "I can feel my soft skin, rough jacket, smooth cold metal chair leg" etc and as I said – really drop your awareness down into the tips of you fingers feeling the item.

3. Things you can hear – as I said before you may have some sensory condition, can't hear or see or smell well – so just swap out one sense for another – this is a guideline only – make all these tools yours! Use that inner dialogue "I can hear muffled traffic outside, a ticking clock, clipped footsteps in the corridor" etc if it's really quiet – move! You can make noise by moving your feet or listen to yourself breathing in deeply etc.

2. What can you Smell? – What aromas are around you, on your skin, clothing, hair if it's long, what about a drink or are you eating?

1. How do you Feel, emotionally? – now this is where you can go online and find this exercise has this last one as the sense of taste, but for me I want to know how I am after I have done the above four, so I am going to sit and ask myself – how do I feel emotionally now? Am I more regulated, am I calmer? If not, I'm going to start back up the top and try again from five things I can see...

Then there's a tool whereby you **pop an alarm on your phone or write a Stick It** (or lots, I love a good brightly coloured Stick It note!) and put in the environments you occupy during the day and every hour or two or three, **take a moment to take a nice deep breath in through the nose** – pause at the very top of the breath, slowly breathe out, like blowing softly on soup (you don't want to splash the person in front of you with that imaginary hot soup!) and do that for one minute. Slow breathing and noticing how that feels in your body. Are there some pockets of tension you could breathe some space around? Give that painful area a bit more space to perhaps start to relax a little?

Or – use that inner voice to recite something, your name, address, DOB, phone number, those of your friends or family, a poem or a song, etc etc. All these things help take the focus off thinking unhelpful and unhealthy thoughts!

Here's a good technique which I find creates some space between you being inside your thoughts and starting to observe them – because it's not our thoughts that create an issue – it's how we behave once we have thought them that creates unhelpful patterns. We only feel emotionally how we do at any given moment by what we are thinking – it's the thought that comes first, then how we feel about the thought and that then creates a behaviour towards ourselves or others. When we start to notice what we are thinking we have far more agency to change the thought out from unhealthy to a healthy thought.

Here's a great technique to do some distancing of your thoughts once you start to notice what you are thinking. And just to say – it's a practice – noticing your thoughts, so don't worry if you are far down the rabbit hole of a familiar unhelpful thought and behaviour when you notice that's what's going on – you can always change things right there and then. And the more you practice something the quicker you will get at realising an unhealthy thought earlier and earlier until – hey presto! – you are about to start the 'I'm not good enough' stuff and you will catch it right there and then and can then challenge it with this:

Try putting in front of an unhelpful or unkind thought:
Oh, I am having the thought that –
...or try distancing yourself even further with...
I notice I am having the thought that...

This tool is part of Cognitive Diffusion in Acceptance and Commitment Therapy (ACT) which you can find out lots about online or in libraries.

Walking – and the benefits of being outside especially if you can be in nature.

Walking does something to the brain; it helps it organise itself and balance out a bit. That's partly due to the act of walking which re- balances the body and therefore the mind by the symmetry of rhythmic left and right movement. Being out in nature does other things too and here's just a few examples:

Walking in trees and nature in general for at least 15 mins – can reduce chemicals including which is one of the hormones which can cause anxiety and depression. So when we walk and breathe in the chemicals which the trees and nature release (these are called phytoncides or easier to remember – 'wood' essential oils) our circulatory system responds by decreasing our blood pressure and calming our nervous system. All this and it boosts our energy as we are moving our bodies and improving circulation and muscle tone.

Wildlife – Birds, mammals & insects – looking for them can be so exciting ~ when we search for & allow ourselves to feel awe at seeing or finding something which is ultimately wild & beautiful ~ our brain release's another feel good hormone, dopamine – which has the nickname of a "chemical hug".

Water – it can be a river, stream, brook or even a water feature in our garden, or a city fountain – listening to the sound of water decreases our cortisol levels (that's a stress hormone) in turn we then feel more relaxed. MRI scans have shown that we move further away from our fight & flight reptilian brain response and move towards relaxation –

it's like a weekend break for our neurons, or longer the more you sit beside/listen to it!

Get your hands in soil – yes really! It has micro-organisms called mycobacterium vaci.
When we smell these micro-organisms a group of neurons in our brain are triggered & release serotonin – one of the positive neurotransmitters and this improves mood – just like the effect of pharmaceutical anti-depressants. (So go on! Sniff that soil! Hands in the earth, digging etc Please do check for animal waste first though!)

Spending time looking at fractal botanical features. This actually lowers our levels of cortisol (that pesky stress hormone) BTW – FRACTAL means the same system but in different sizes; think of a fern or a house leek plant (Sempervivum). Staring at fractal features activates the same areas of brain which light up when we listen to uplifting music which, as we all feel – music we love is SO mood effective, especially if you can boogie along to something as well as listening to it!

I mentioned **dancing to a fav tune** – but also singing loudly or humming softly also is really beneficial to the Vagus Nerve (look it up – Very important part of the nervous system and best kept calm as much as possible as it wanders through all your major organs between head and gut, so has a massive impact on the functioning of your systems like digestion, detoxifying etc) Humming is one of the things which calms it down, as well as splashing your face with cold water, but it also likes a good feel tune to whistle and jig along to!

Then there's the self-care stuff I am sure you have already come across

A special bath with a smell you love, maybe candles (keep safe and don't fall asleep in there or knock off lit flames!)

Being really well hydrated – if you aren't this can have a massive impact on how you think and feel

Eating regularly and food closest to the sun. What I mean by that is fresh foods and not highly processed, but I know you know this stuff!

Getting regular and if you can sufficient sleep and when you can't not fretting about it, but lying still and knowing you are resting your body which is great.

Or listening to theta brain wave music to help you rest and fall asleep (theta is our just before sleep brainwave, it's a super relaxed state to be in!)

Or listening to relaxation music (same thing really)

And staying interested in your future and plans for it

Illustration by T

Worcester Community Trust

Worcester Community Trust is a registered charity that runs six community hubs in the City of Worcester; providing crucial facilities for community use, as well as activities and services that empower people of all ages, including the socially isolated, the lonely, victims of domestic abuse and the wider community.

They run a several community projects across these hubs, including the JOY Project – a service which celebrates women's individual journeys and provides support to enable women to gain a variety of skills; and the DAWN Project – a free confidential service for women who have or are experiencing domestic abuse.

What is JOY?
JOY is a female and identifying-only community project which provides support to enable women to access new skills, enhance confidence and empower them to make their own informed choices and decisions. They help women to achieve goals, make friendships and gain new skills and confidence along the way. Each woman's journey will be unique and specifically tailored to their own abilities and needs. They bring women together in a safe environment to improve self-confidence, resilience and develop peer groups who support each other. Referrals are accepted from statutory and voluntary agencies, Police and GPs. Self referrals are also accepted.

Women from both of these groups were involved in the creation of Unheard Voices: Our Journey to Joy project.

www.worcestercommunitytrust.org.uk

Like what you read?

Why not get involved?

We run funded writing workshops, courses and writing for wellbeing events throughout Worcestershire and beyond, and over online platforms. Feel free to email to express your interest and we'll add you to our mailing list. Alternatively, follow us on facebook and instagram: @thewordassociationcic

Part of a community group, charity or organisation who might benefit from a writing session or course? Please do get in touch and see how we can work with you. Our facilitators have experience of working with young people, vulnerable adults, at risk children, those battling addiction, offenders and survivors of sexual abuse and domestic violence.

Email info@the-word-association.com to express your interest.

www.the-word-association.com

Support Us

Thank you for your interest in this book. We hope you feel inspired, educated and curious by what you have read.

We have plans to deliver many more writing programmes and produce many more anthologies with the LGBTQ+ community, people with mental health needs and survivors of sexual abuse and domestic violence. To keep our work free for our participants and audiences, we rely on funding. If you love our work and are able to contribute a small donation, we can use it towards our next project!

Thank you so much

https://ko-fi.com/thewordassociation

Cover art by Nashmin Riazi

I live in England but am originally from Iran. I'm an abstract and expressionist artist. I have been painting for over 27 years and started off as a realist painter.

As a little girl, I used to draw on anything I could see. On my hands, on my face, on the walls of the house, later on the class bench and on the blackboard with white chalk or coloured chalks, on the school floor, etc. Seeing my love for painting, my mother sent me to painting classes. Later, when I grew up, I learned realistic nature painting from several renowned teachers.

Later, I was admitted to university for Art, but due to the revolution in my country and the political situation, I was not allowed to study academically!

I immigrated to Germany and learned fabric dyeing and design in a fabric factory in Hannover. Later, I emigrated from Germany to England and learned painting with the figures of live models. All this helped me to learn the creation of space, textures and patterns in the work of painting. I was a realistic painter until 2016, when I met and fell in love with the abstract painting style.

My familiarity with the abstract style pushed me to another world. The imaginary and unreal world that my mind was always searching for. Illustrating with colour and sometimes combining different materials made me aware of the creativity inside and I use it for my paintings. In addition to my interest in illustrating and colour, I believe painting activates my creativity and my awareness. I love the shapes and colours that appear naturally when I let my mind run free.

I've exhibited my work in different parts of the world such as England, Iran and Spain and continue to work on my craft daily.